R is for Rugby

An Alphabet Book

N is for Nola!

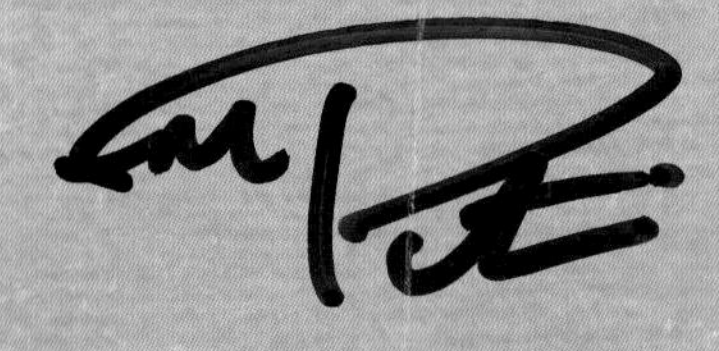

Written by Mike Petri
Illustrations by Max Thompson

For
Lauren & Evie

R is for rugby,
a gentleman's game.
A school boy in England
gave rugby its fame.

This alphabet book
will look at each letter
to help understand
the sport a bit better.

Anthem

With hand over heart,
it's a time to be proud.
We all stand as one
and together sing loud.

Ball

The ball for this sport
is an odd, funny shape.
It is oval not round,
it resembles a grape!

C

Cap

A cap is awarded
when playing a test.
It's small and embroidered
with the national crest.

D

Drop goal

A difficult kick,
the ball drops on its nose.
It bounces back up
and is struck with your toes!

Eight

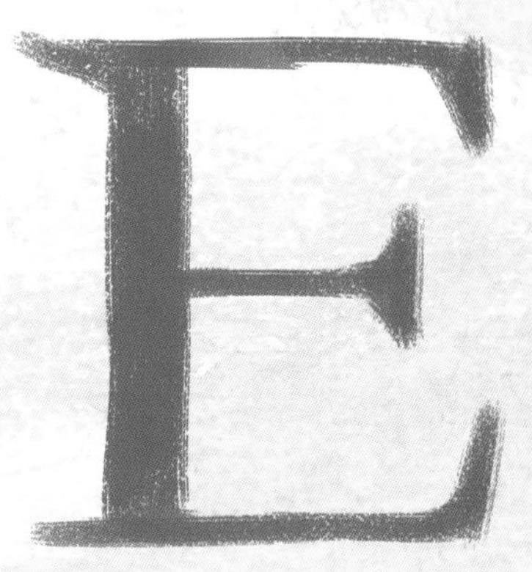

The base of the scrum,
he wears number eight.
He runs like a bull
and tackles just great!

Fly-half

This number ten
is a jack of all trades.
He can run, pass, or kick
while he calls all the plays.

G

Grubber

G is for grubber.
It's a kick on the ground,
quite tricky to catch
as it bounces around!

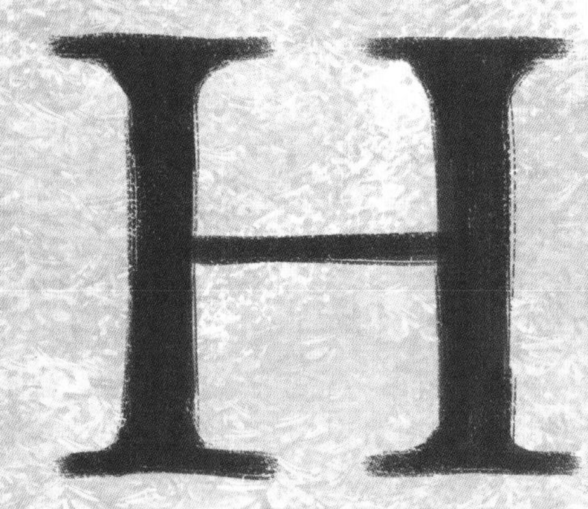

Hooker

**In front of the pack,
without using hands,
they hook the ball back
as fast as they can.**

I

Inside Center

One of two centers
that work as a pair
patrolling the middle,
so runners beware!

J

Jersey

Known for the stripes
and also the collar,
the patch on the chest
is a symbol of honor.

Kicker

Set the ball on a tee
and take a step back.
Line up the angle
and give it a whack!

L

Lineout

The ball is thrown in
when it goes out of bounds.
They lift the tall locks
way up off the ground.

M

Maul

In this type of play
ruggers stay on their feet,
pushing together
as opponents retreat.

N

Nine

The scrum-half is the link
between forwards and backs.
He wears number nine
and starts the attack.

Offload

In the midst of a tackle
at the end of a run,
toss to a mate
and continue the fun!

Prop

The numbers they wear
are a one or a three.
Each giant prop
is as big as a tree!

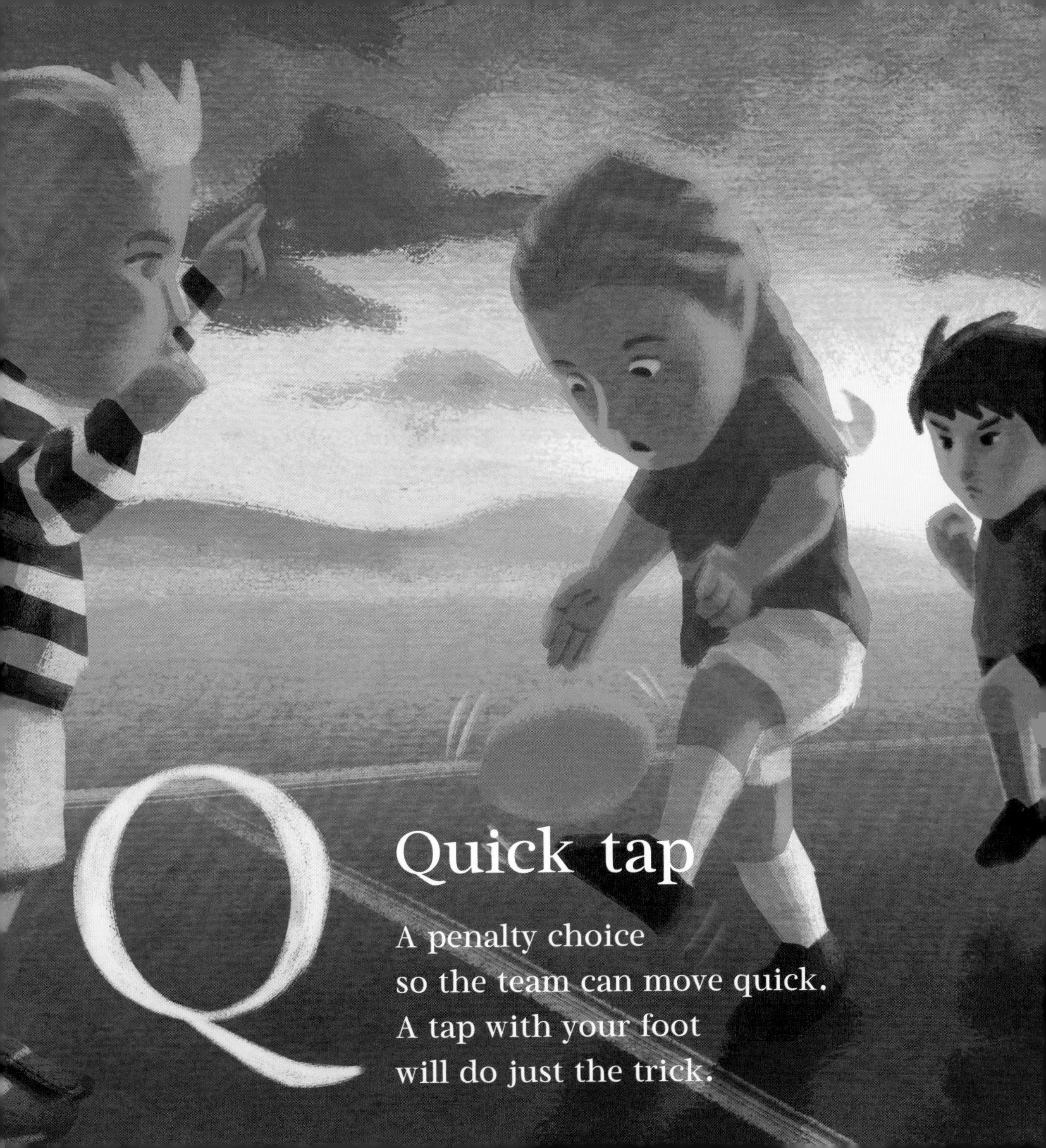

Q

Quick tap

A penalty choice
so the team can move quick.
A tap with your foot
will do just the trick.

R

Ruck

When a runner goes down
he may seem to be stuck,
but play does not stop
they instead form a ruck!

S

Scrum

It's a synchronized push
to compete for the ball.
"Crouch, bind, and set."
Engage on this call.

T

Try

Cross over the line,
touch the ball down to score.
Five points on the board
and hear the crowd roar!

U

Up and Under

This type of kick
goes up very high.
Up, up, and away
it soars in the sky.

V

Victory

No matter who wins,
cheer "hip, hip, hooray!"
Opponents shake hands
for a great game today.

Wing

W

Fast as a cheetah
these wingers can fly,
showing her speed
racing in for a try.

X

X–play

The most basic play
is an old fashioned switch.
One player will strike,
but it's tough to tell which.

Yellow card

Sometimes a player
does something unfair.
Sin bin for ten minutes
alone in a chair.

Zig-zag

The fullback is quick,
he will zig and then zag.
He scurries around
like a fast game of tag!

R is for rugby
but it doesn't stop there.
This wonderful sport
is a game we should share!

P is for PETRI

Mike Petri is a professional rugby player and team captain for Rugby United New York in Major League Rugby. He's earned over 50 test caps for the USA Eagles National Team and has represented the USA in three Rugby World Cup tournaments. He's won national championships with New York Athletic Club and Belmont Shore, been featured for the prestigious Barbarians international side, and played professionally in the UK for Sale Sharks and Newport Dragons. While studying at Xavier High School in New York City, Mike played for the USA U19 National Team in two Junior World Championships and went on to be a four time College All American at Penn State University.

Mike's rugby family spans far and wide, but he lives with his wife and two daughters in Brooklyn, New York, where he is a high school teacher and youth coach. Passionate about growing the game, Mike wrote R is for Rugby as way to share the sport he loves with his kids and with kids around the world. Through this book, he hopes to inspire a new generation of rugby fans, players, and families.

R is for Rugby: An Alphabet Book is Mike's debut children's book but there is much more in store! Visit our website for more rugby fun!

RisforRugby.com

RUGBY WORLD CUP 2015

USA RUGBY

First published by Augusto 2014.
www.augusto.co.nz

Written by Mike Petri
Illustrations by Max Thompson
Design layout by Louise Kellerman & Dan Gearity

ISBN Number: 978-0-9863653-0-0

Printed in the USA.